Mystery Socks

Loretta Haynes

ISBN 979-8-88540-125-8 (paperback)
ISBN 979-8-88540-126-5 (digital)

Christian Faith Publishing
832 Park Avenue
Meadville, PA 16335
www.christianfaithpublishing.com

Printed in the United States of America

Mystery Socks

Loretta Haynes

On a breezy fall night, my mom said, "Buddy, Buddy, please find all of your socks. I cannot find them. I cannot find them.

"I cannot find them," I said.

We cannot find them, not even under your bed. Are the socks flying somewhere in the air? Or are they even behind the chairs? I have looked in Chester's drawers and closets, you see. Could you have buried them under the tall, tall trees?

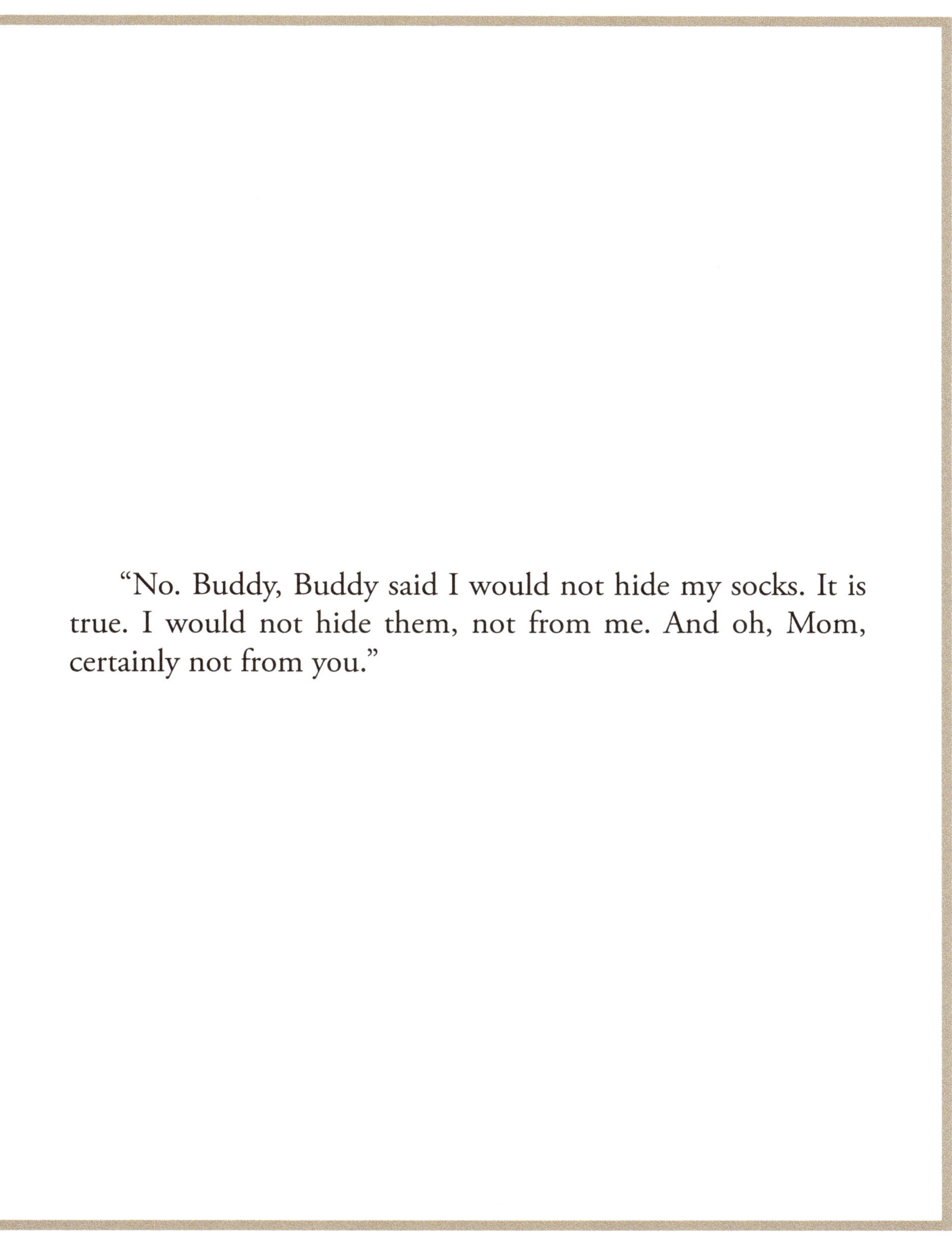

"No. Buddy, Buddy said I would not hide my socks. It is true. I would not hide them, not from me. And oh, Mom, certainly not from you."

The sock! The sock! I always have one, but the other socks just seems to be gone. I will become super sock finder, the best in the land. I will find the other socks. This is getting out of hand.

So I get up early in the morning, and I look all around. But the matching socks just cannot be found.

My sister Izzy and I looked in the bathroom and all over the floor. We looked behind my pillows and the doors. It is time for me to become the super sock finder with my sock cape and mask. This is a real problem, but I will handle the task.

We went outside, and Izzy dug and got down on her knees. I shake and shake and shake the trees. Oh where, oh where, can the other socks be? Are they having a party? Have they ran away from me? I will not give up because I am super sock finder, you see. Those socks will not see the last of me.

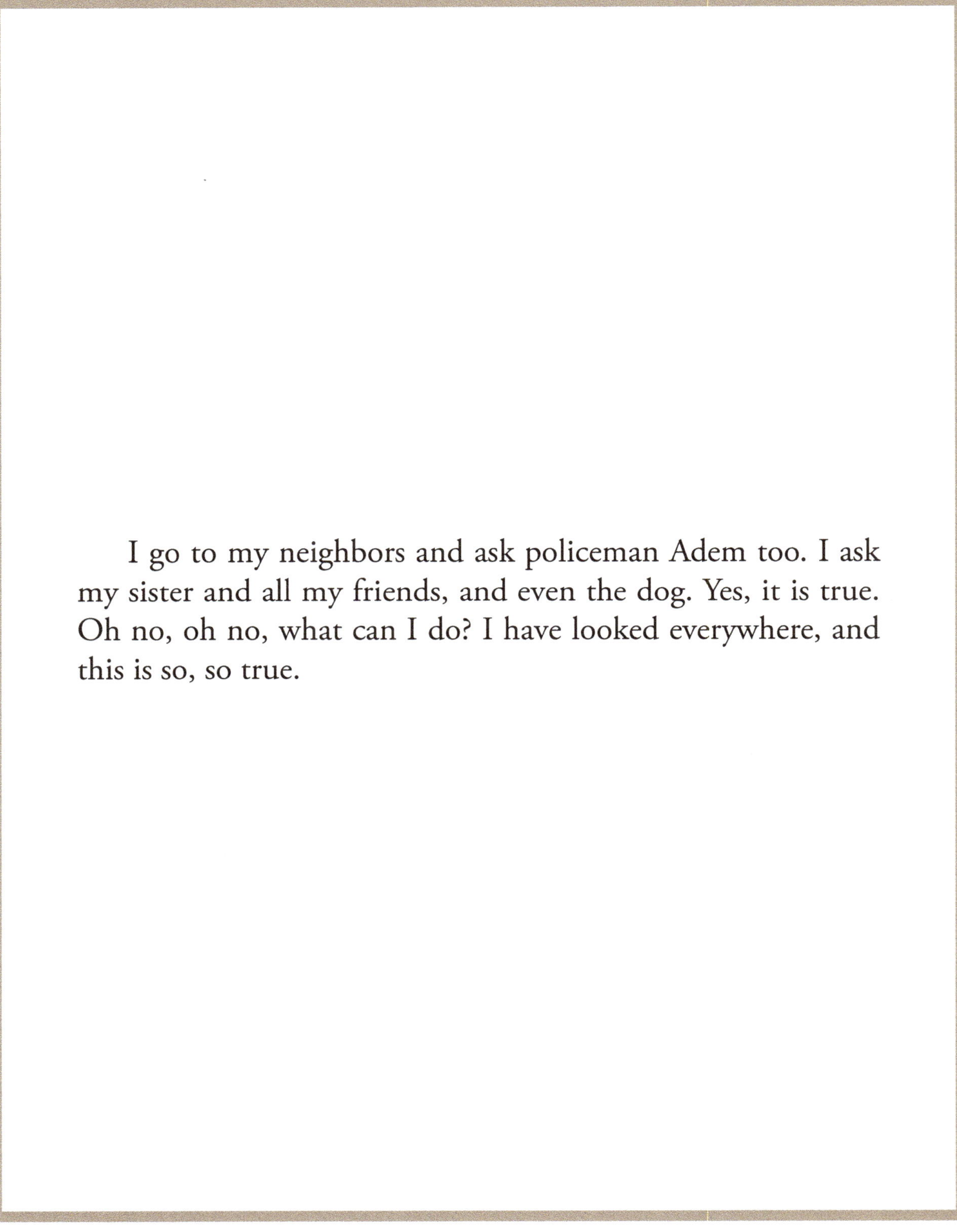

I go to my neighbors and ask policeman Adem too. I ask my sister and all my friends, and even the dog. Yes, it is true. Oh no, oh no, what can I do? I have looked everywhere, and this is so, so true.

Buddy, Buddy, holding his head down starts to cry. Those socks are gone with a tear in my eye.

Then that very night I heard something so strange. It sounded like a party, and it seem to call my name. I slowly opened the dryer and yelled, "Hurray, hurray! The mates of my socks were all here to stay. To this day I wonder how my matching socks appeared. It does not matter now because they are all right here.

About the Author

The author is a preschool teacher of thirty-seven years in which most of those years have been with Southern Illinois University. Her growth and joy of teaching helped her to learn that her storytelling and writing of stories was key in children's learning and development.

Her nickname is Buttons, which was given to her by her dad, who she dearly loves and cherishes. She is a mother of three, two boys and a girl. Their names are Latisha, Lamario, and Delano. She has eight beautiful grandchildren: Kevin, Bernard, Jason, Delano Jr., Isabel Nichole, Mario Jr., Angelica, and Luis. They are the loves of her life. Most of all she is so thankful for her parents, Delores and Richard Fulton. They are truly her life and her inspiration.

What she realized was that telling stories to children was a window to learning, language development, and creativity. Telling stories helps to enhance children's cognitive, physical, and emotional development. She has so much enjoyment in telling, singing, and writing stories for children and families.

The inspiration for writing her book, *Mystery Socks*, came about when they were having a sock hop at school and the children wanted her to tell a story; and that is how *Mystery Socks* was born. She hopes that this book brings joy, learning, and laughter to all.

Her book is about learning and developing social skills. Also her book is about learning and having fun while reading. So enjoy solving this wonderful mystery together.